We Are All

We All Play

Rebecca Rissman

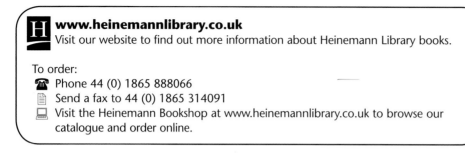

www.heinemannlibrary.co.uk

Visit our website to find out more information about Heinemann Library books.

To order:

☎ Phone 44 (0) 1865 888066

▤ Send a fax to 44 (0) 1865 314091

▣ Visit the Heinemann Bookshop at www.heinemannlibrary.co.uk to browse our catalogue and order online.

Heinemann Library is an imprint of Capstone Global Library Limited, a company incorporated in England and Wales having its registered office at 7 Pilgrim Street, London, EC4V 6LB – Registered company number: 6695582

Heinemann is a registered trademark of Pearson Education Limited, under licence to Capstone Global Library Limited

Edited by Rebecca Rissman, Charlotte Guillain and Catherine Veitch
Designed by Joanna Hinton-Malivoire
Picture research by Tracy Cummins
Production by Duncan Gilbert
Originated by Dot Gradations Ltd
Printed and bound in China by South China Printing Company Ltd

ISBN 978 0 431 19309 0 (hardback)
13 12 11 10 09
10 9 8 7 6 5 4 3 2 1

ISBN 978 0 431 19315 1 (paperback)
14 13 12 11 10
10 9 8 7 6 5 4 3 2 1

British Library Cataloguing in Publication Data
Rissman, Rebecca
We all play. - (We are all different)
1. People with disabilities - Juvenile literature 2. Play - Juvenile literature
305.9'08
A full catalogue record for this book is available from the British Library.

Acknowledgements
We would like to thank the following for permission to reproduce photographs: ©agefotostock p. **4** (John Birdsall); ©Corbis pp. **7** (zefa/Mika), **14** (Reuters/Claro Cortes IV); ©drr.net pp. **12** (Leah Warkentin), **15** (Janine Wiedel), **18** (Leah Warkentin); ©Getty Images pp. **6** (Tara Moore), **8** (Brent Stirton), **9** (Siri Stafford), **10** (Robert Prezioso), **11** (Gary Buss), **12** (NBAE/D. Clarke Evans), **19** (Michael Cogliantry), **20** (Realistic Reflections), **21** (Celia Peterson), **23 top** (Realistic Reflections), **23 middle** (Brent Stirton), **23 bottom** (Robert Prezioso/Getty Images); ©Shutterstock pp. **13** (Koer), **16** (Damir Karan), **17** (Loesevsky Pavel), **22** (M W Productions).

Cover photograph of a basketball training session in Burkina Faso reproduced with permission of ©Corbis (Andy Aitchison). Back cover photograph of children playing football reproduced with permission of ©Getty Images (Siri Stafford).

Every effort has been made to contact copyright holders of material reproduced in this book. Any omissions will be rectified in subsequent printings if notice is given to the publishers.

Disclaimer
All the Internet addresses (URLs) given in this book were valid at the time of going to press. However, due to the dynamic nature of the Internet, some addresses may have changed, or sites may have changed or ceased to exist since publication. While the author and Publishers regret any inconvenience this may cause readers, no responsibility for any such changes can be accepted by either the author or the Publishers.

Contents

Differences

We are all different ages and sizes. We all have different coloured hair and skin. We are all good at different things.

Playing

When we play we can learn
new things.

When we play we can have fun.

When we play we can explore.
This man is using crutches to help him.

When we play we can exercise.

We can play many different sports.

How we play

Sometimes we play games with a ball.
Some people use a wheelchair to play.

Sometimes we build things when we play. People can build with sand on the beach.

Sometimes people play in a team.
This team is playing basketball.

Sometimes people play on their own.
This girl is blowing bubbles.

Sometimes people play with a partner. This girl is playing table tennis with a partner.

Sometimes people play in a club.
These children are playing
music together.

Sometimes people play
computer games.

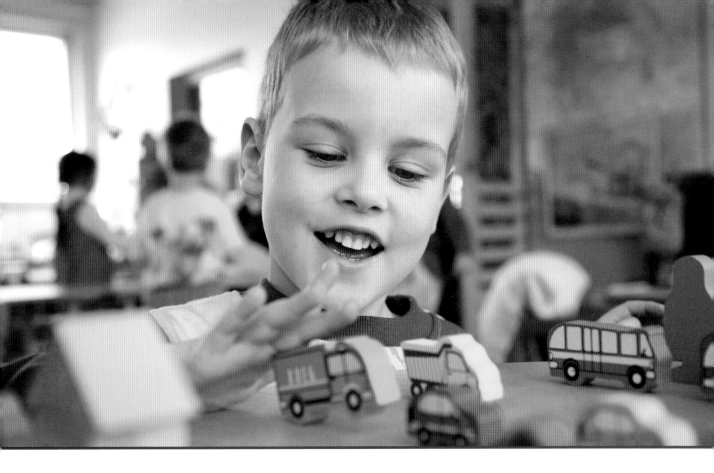

Sometimes people play with toys.

Where we play

Sometimes people play outside.
People play with skateboards outside.

Sometimes people play inside. Many people play music inside.

Children play at school. This girl is using a brace to help her play.

People play at home. These children are playing in the garden.

We are all different

There are many different ways of playing. Which do you like best?

Words to know

brace something people wear to help them grow and move

crutches long poles that some people use to walk

wheelchair chair with wheels. Some people use wheelchairs to get around and play sport.

Index

Note to parents and teachers

Before reading
Encourage the children to think of the ways that they are different from one another. Then explain that being different makes everyone special. Ask the children to form pairs. Ask them to talk to a partner and to tell each other their favourite game. Then ask each partner to tell you what their partner likes to play. Collect in the answers and list them under sports, board games, music, computer games, and playground games on the board.

After reading
Tell the children to look through magazines and catalogues and to cut out pictures of people playing sports, music, or games. Make a collage of these pictures and help the children to write labels for each activity. Then lead children in a discussion about the many ways that people can play.